T0195988

MY SPECIAL BOOTS

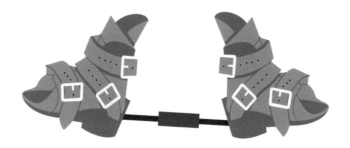

By Margaret A. White
Illustrations by Lucie Rice

Copyright © 2021 Margaret A. White.

All rights reserved. No part of this book may be used or reproduced by any means, graphic, electronic, or mechanical, including photocopying, recording, taping or by any information storage retrieval system without the written permission of the author except in the case of brief quotations embodied in critical articles and reviews.

This book is a work of non-fiction. Unless otherwise noted, the author and the publisher make no explicit guarantees as to the accuracy of the information contained in this book and in some cases, names of people and places have been altered to protect their privacy.

Archway Publishing books may be ordered through booksellers or by contacting:

Archway Publishing
1663 Liberty Drive
Bloomington, IN 47403
www.archwaypublishing.com
844-669-3957

Because of the dynamic nature of the Internet, any web addresses or links contained in this book may have changed since publication and may no longer be valid. The views expressed in this work are solely those of the author and do not necessarily reflect the views of the publisher, and the publisher hereby disclaims any responsibility for them.

Any people depicted in stock imagery provided by Getty Images are models, and such images are being used for illustrative purposes only.
Certain stock imagery © Getty Images.

Interior Image Credit: Lucie Rice

ISBN: 978-1-6657-0117-4 (sc)
ISBN: 978-1-6657-0116-7 (e)

Print information available on the last page.

Archway Publishing rev. date: 02/25/2021

ARCHWAY
PUBLISHING

ACKNOWLEDGEMENTS

For our "super hero" Teagan who has taught us so much about joy and perseverance and our incredible Allyson and Colinson who help lead Teagan through this life every day. I love you all more than you'll ever know. For my mother who helped me put the notes to the tune! You are wonderful! For Great Mimi and Grandpa Ed as angels who have guided me. For my beautiful husband for his dedication and all of his love and support. You have brought us so far! You are amazing!

I can do all things in Christ who strengthens me. Philippians 4:13 NKJV

"The sun is down and time for bed!"
This is what my Mommy said...

I look for my shoes,
they are fun you see.

They are made especially for me!

They help me to grow big and strong

and heal my feet so I can play all day long.

My boots, they help me walk.

My boots, they help me run.

Oh how I love my special bootsies.

My boots, they help me walk.

My boots, they help me run.

Oh how I love my special bootsies.

The doctors said when I was born,
my feet were special too.

They made these boots
to help me grow,

so my feet would feel like new!

When I wake up, it's time to stretch and stand.
No more shoes until it's bedtime again.

My feet feel strong, I can move all day.

I thank God for my shoes and doctors so I can run and play.

SING ALONG TO
MY SPECIAL BOOTS

My boots, they help me walk. My boots, they help me run.

Oh how I love my special boot sies.

My boots, they help me walk. My boots, they help me run.

Oh how I love my special boot sies.

The doc tor said when I was born,

my feet were special too!

They made these boots to help me grow,

so my feet would feel like new!

Margaret A. White is a mother of three, former educator who understands both the challenges and beauties of disabilities. She has experienced both the fear and anxieties as both a patient with disabilities and now a mother of a son who has come so far in just his first four years of life. Margaret's mission in sharing this story is to provide both peace and hope to future parents and patients who face disabilities while providing insight and resources from a well-known pediatric surgeon, Dr. Randall Loder, from Riley Hospital in Indianapolis, IN. Her goal is to spread the word around the globe about the need for education and resources so that the thousands of children and adults who have been born with clubbed feet know that there is an option that provides hope and healing.

Many children all over the world are diagnosed with clubfoot each year and still today, in the year 2021, some of these same children do not have access to the treatment that has become the number one treatment for treating and correcting the deformity. The Ponseti Method is a procedure that was pioneered and practiced by Spanish-born American physician Dr. Ignacio Ponseti in the 1940s while practicing at the University of Iowa Health Center. The Ponseti Method became more wildly sought out by the use of the Internet in the 1990s. The Ponseti Method is a procedure consisting of a series of gentle repositioning and casting of the foot. After 6 to 8 weeks, a small procedure to lengthen the Achilles tendon is often required. Children are then fitted for special shoes attached to a brace to be worn up to 4 years. The Ponseti Method is known to be successful in up to 89 percent of patients who do not require surgery.

Dr. Randall T. Loder, who specializes in Pediatric Orthopedic Surgery at Riley Children's Hospital in Indianapolis, IN, was practicing the Radical Release Method when in 2003 he made the decision to drive to Iowa City to attend the Seminars held by Dr. Ponseti himself to learn the Ponseti Method technique. Dr. Loder has been practicing the Ponseti Method ever since and insists that the Ponseti Method is by far the better option over Radial Release for patients and believes in the success rate. As a specialist and well-known pediatric surgeon, Loder has stated the Ponseti Method can be very affordable and successful with limited resources. He along with many others, hope to see the education of Ponseti Method become known and available all over the world.

For further information, please refer to the following resources...

POSNA.org

Orthokids.org/Condition/Clubfoot

Miraclefeet.org

britannica.com/biography/Ignacio-Vives-Ponseti

Printed in the United States
By Bookmasters